# GREENS OF JUNE

by Taylor Jade

© 2021, Greens of June

All rights reserved. No part of this publication may be reproduced, distributed, or transmitted in any form by any means, including photocopying, recording, or other methods without the prior written permission of the author, except in the case of brief quotations embodied in reviews and certain other noncommercial uses permitted by copyright law. For permission requests, write to the author at the address below.

Taylor Jade
justtaylorjade@gmail.com

ISBN: 978-0-578-86933-9

Printed in the United States of America

A book of heart songs,
heartaches,
desires,
destruction,
rebuild,
rejoice
and so on...

Welcome to my brain on words.
Take your shoes off at the door.

## TABLE OF CONTENTS:

1. JADED .................. 1
2. WATER GIRL ................ 27
3. EBB & FLOW ................ 53
4. THE PROCESS (of You) ........... 79
5. CREATOR ................... 105
6. LOVE LANGUAGE ................ 131
7. GARDEN ................... 157
8. HOME ................... 183

After all this time
I finally realized
everything I wrote for Them
was always meant
to be read by You.

My soul pre-prepared me for your arrival.


-Forward Thinking

# JADED

I am layered...
Each level of me
is important
to my wholeness.

Do you possess the depth
within yourself
to dig through my complexities?

How strong
is your resilience
when the ground is shaking?

Can you hold on
-or better yet-
hold within
the strength
which brings forth
softness?

**He used to tell me
I only wanted him so I could
have him as a trophy...**

Little did he know,
he was right.

He was the greatest prize, to me.

I felt like I could always see a world of possibility in him
but he couldn't even get a glimpse of it.

Does Disneyland know it's Disneyland?

Does it know how many people it unites in one place,
for the good of everyone?

Does he know he's my Disneyland?

The way he makes me feel like a kid again,
seeing colors a little brighter
and a heart wide-open...

Season passes are expensive these days,
but I guess the people
who truly want to be there
will make that kind of investment.

Only the people who understand its joy
will give what they need
to get inside.

**Thoughts that never turned to words...**

The 10am ones.
The 2pm ones.
The 10pm ones.
The 2am ones...

I swear my brain designated those times to thoughts of you...
You're turning into a bad habit.

I wish I could unscrew your cap and let free
everything that is trapped.

There's always something missing with you.

Maybe it's stuck behind a jail cell
made of clenched teeth...

Relax your jaw,
release your mind my love.

There's so much we could explore
and time isn't available for wasting.

We have dreams to catch
but our baggage weighs as anchors
and we're stuck again...

Grounded.

Empty your bags,
take off and collect
the new that you find
along the way...

The subject changed,
but here I am
still thinking of you.

I don't work a 9-5
but most of the time
I'm giving you 95
and receiving less than 59...

You wouldn't even pass on a good day,
but here I am giving you all the answers;
feeding you with the cleanest silver spoon I have
and building you up
so you can build everyone else up...

And still,
I'll do the dishes.

While you're out there
saving the world
I'm praying
I save myself
so we can meet each other at the top.

...And here I am again with your silver spoon.

One day I'll find a King who shares his meals.

**Dishwasher**

He was the only thing
that could both tear me apart
and hold me so close together
you would've never known
there were cracks in the foundation...

He meant well,
even when he didn't.
There wasn't a bone in his body
that wasn't touched by love.

It's not every day you get blessed by an angel,
even when it's fallen...

He made me feel
emotions that were
virgin to me
and I became
more of a woman
the more I watched him
discover new pieces of man
inside of himself,
sparked from words I breathed into him...

He gave me a reason
to breathe more life into myself.

My breath doesn't feel shallow anymore.

Today I pray for the strength of us both..
We had let time make a fool of us
and constantly lived by clocks with loose screws...

We didn't have the right tools at hand,
so used to the pivot...

Now we're facing backwards.

**-Consequences of Father Time**

**Do you still desire to know me?**
I see your brows take shape at the sight of me...
I've never seen it before.

Lost...
Like I gave you direction in Braille.

Although I crave your fingertips knowing every inch of me,
I can still use my words out loud to guide you...

But do you want to go there?

To unleash the "why's" and "how's" of my existence;
if you asked, I'm dying to tell you.
I'd probably shed old skin
and generate new before your eyes.
Sometimes conversation is the backbone of healing.

But are you tired?

Maybe I could come back when you're well-rested.
I inhale the sound of your breath while sleeping,
sometimes I hear "I love you" during exhale.

Is it the last of it you have to give?
I don't want to drain you.

This territory is new for the both of us.
We aren't used to long holds on soul-ties,
we're used to convenience and concocted chaos.

I swear all the prayers towards other men
were meant for you.

...

God heard me wailing for love without question
and you gave that...

Now here we are,
a mark.

**What once was exclamation,
changed punctuation through time.**

From what I hear,
it's normal.

I want to spend a lifetime of
commas and run-on sentences with you.

Do you have the capacity in your lungs to give air that long?

I am patient enough to wait and see...

Period.

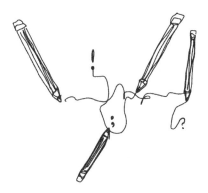

**From the eyes of a dragon**
**our love dragged on**
**the way fairytales do...**

We were Romeo and Juliet.
Our love for each other was true,
but toxic in the way
that we couldn't see past our differences...
They made a difference.

We breathed fire;
both in passionate moments
and in times
when it spewed from our tongues
like we were the beast itself.

Back full of knives
like the spikes on the spine
of a 30-foot monster.

And yet... we were enthralled in mysticism.
An elusive force pulled us back and forth
and mistook high guards for shining armor...

I wish we would stop romanticizing fairytales.

Now I'm here,
and I see you;
pretending to protect me
while I'm wishing I was you...

Free.

The castle around me crumbled.

We live in a world
of "what's next's"
and "what now's"

A world where
attention spans
can be limited to
60 seconds or less
and being accepted
is verified
with a double tap.
Every day feels the same
in the need to be
drastically different...

We spend so much time
pushing forward
while simultaneously
wishing for time
to slow down...
To feel all the changes
without feeling
overwhelmed by it.

I am calling on the present
to grasp onto me
and anchor me down.
Ground me in the process
of my blessings.
Don't let anything go untouched,
unthanked
or unloved...

**Life,
give me all of you.**

How ironic it is
to come to the conclusion that
things were much more simple
during the complicated times...

Before it was unacceptable
to be anything
but an expectation.

Before a mind had to mold
to fit into a perspective
outside of its own...

What good is a solution
to a problem that doesn't want to be solved?
That in which
the addition of division
multiplies the chances
of complete subtraction
of ourselves
from the equation.

**Things were simpler when it was complicated.**

When thoughts were shaped differently,
spit out in comfortability,
received with vulnerability,
and the desire to understand
what wasn't understood
was the rawest feeling of tranquility.

**Naked in unjudged truth,
I felt comfortable sharing my scars with you...**

If your fingers traced my skin,
goosebumps would replace old wounds
and remind me that love
is the perfect place for healing.

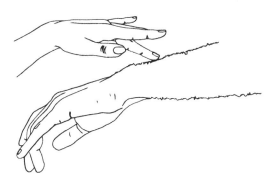

There were many things
I was required to take the fall for
when it came to you...

But the only thing
that made it fair for me

was guaranteeing
that you'd be falling with me.

I'm sorry that
we're so used to
cuts and bruises
that we never thought twice
about taking
the leap...

**I'm glad that we're
both back to safety.**

**I couldn't help it...
I found the holes
in your perfection.**

Digging,
deeply inserting
two fingers into
what I saw as
blank space.

I increased it, bigger.
My awareness perceived
obstacles as thicker
and there they went...

I always do this to myself,
turn people into pedestals.

They never measure up...

It was all an illusion,
your size.
And there was nothing
more to blame
than these eyes...

Battling what I feel
and what I see,
the ego is compromised.

I still want every part of you...

And what about you, for me?

Today is a battlefield
of soldiers
armed for war,
prepared to attack and defend
at any hint of foreign movement.

Unmasked,
we fight for the same triumph-

to be loved unconditionally
and become veteran to violence.

**But here we are,**
**blinded by our own revolution...**

I hope one day
we realize that these are sacred grounds;
that only those
guided by the light of love
can pass through without fatality...

That all things driven by that force
will pave the way to healing for the lost ones

and maybe then,
we will meet again
on the path to unquestioned liberation.

I hope to see you there.

I don't want to fight
I just want to be...

Lay down your weapon,
we are on the same team.

**-Cut by a double-edged sword.**

**When I place my faith
in the hands of a human,
I find myself
quickly disappointed.**

Our hands are messy,
loose grips and sweaty palms
plague opportunity
on tight holds
and healthy soul-ties.
I do my best to find the God in them.
Free-will
fucks with true freedom.
Blinded...
Where did we consciously let go of
proper communication
and respect for self
so deep
that every interaction
was direct reflection
of true character.
Come correct,
stand up straight.
Every person you meet
deserves the lifted-chin
version of you.
Who are you to behave otherwise?
There are angels
counting on you
for divine intervention.
You just may be
the person
who saves the world
through the hands of a human...

Strengthen your grip.

I spent twice
the needed time
doubling back
over bridges
that should've been burned
100 times.

**How many times
do we really need to learn
the same lesson?**

Sometimes I wish
I could put my heart in a cage...
With barriers snug enough to hold it into place,
but soft enough
to provide cushion during turbulence.

Maybe its passion
wouldn't cross barriers
and barge into roped-off territories
out of need to be heard.

And maybe
it would be far enough
out of reach
to not be damaged by those
who aren't warranted a key...

Although I truly know
that it'd worsen the case,
Sometimes I wish
I could put my heart in a cage...

**-2 birds, 1 stone**

Sometimes I wish my heart was caged
for all the times I'm filled with rage
and take my feelings out, not right
it's hard to feel the love in spite.


Sometimes I wish my heart was caged
for all the times my love was staged.
I never would have seen the show,
but now I have the seeds to grow.


I thought I wished my heart was caged...
The little bird had learned to graze
on feed that would decrease her might,
so home in a cage, is no longer in sight...


**-Blackbird**

You used to come over at 2am
and fulfilled all my cravings in the sweetest way...
**You never had to touch me,
but your words did.**

I miss my soul food.

Everything about you was Home,
especially the way
you always
left the light on for me.

I swear there was never a dull moment...
Not even in your pointless tales
that always kept me interested
just because
they made your eyes glisten loud
in quiet moments..

I miss my dream chaser.

Now when it's dark and I travel far,
I close my eyes
but Home isn't where the heart is
because my heart is stuck on you
and your light burned out
for me...

And I keep coming back with broken bulbs
trying to make them work because
I just want you to see the light in me
and my hands are bleeding...

You just want your own light.

Well that makes 2 of us.

Nothing will ever feel the same
or right
or comfortable
when we are not together.

We are two souls,
drawn back from a past life of love
again defeated
by this physical realm...

You were familiar before I even got to know you.
Your arms molded around me to hold
the first time we made plan
and since that day,
any arms outside of yours
just feel like
t a k e n   u p   s p a c e.

**Now this is the moment of truth.**
**The proof of my love for you...**

The letting go
in faith of coming back,
but content in knowing
even if you never find me again,
at least you found you.

**I've written many letters
on the paper in my head**

on the things I wish to say,
what I loved
and now regret...

It feels like wasted time,
getting up
and pushing through;
when today you're 'sposed to be here,
and I'm back,
stranger to you.

I know the way life works,
new beginnings
and release...

And the letters written to you
get replaced
by letters
written to me.

# WATER GIRL

**The truth is that
I love you SO much**
that I'm afraid
that if I finally
let the words
leave my lips
I'll never be able
to stop letting it
burst into moments
like a roaring tide
when it ravages through
a flood gate;
breaking into
unfiltered moments-
full of cleanse,
but destructive
with intensity...
I don't want you to become
yet another victim
to be swept up in
the depths of me.

**You asked me**
    **-put me-**
**in a higher stage of responsibility;**
claimed me as your own
so that I would be
no one else's
and then revoked my privilege
of having fulfilled needs...
Remember that
the retrogrades will always
pull you backwards
to re-introduce you to
old ways
to bring new patterns to...
I am not myself that was
a year ago
but I am a person who
learns more about
the importance of running forward
to balance the current
which tries to sway me
in opposition-
I have swam in this ocean before.
    I am a woman of the sea.
Depth doubles as a middle name
and promise of force.
I am not to be
waded in
but swam alongside
in perfect alignment
so not to get
caught up in ourselves...
I will either
nourish you or
drown you.

    ...

Regardless of choice,
I am destined
to strengthen...
To love me
is to love a work-out;
an exercise
of durability
and additional ability
to ride the tides
outside of your own-
      I require deep attention
to the details
big and small...
To know the surface of the waves
and the fine foundation
of the ocean floor
which motions every move;
to study the life
which lives inside me
and claims me as their home...
Who gets nourished by
my hospitality
and relies on me
for growth.
You are far from
the only one
dependent on
my consistent duty
to show up.
      -But still-
I'll find a way
to give direct
focus to you...
      I'll distill myself,
filter out the salt
to quench the needs
you long for...

...

I am a woman of the ocean.
I am mighty
but I'm soft.
Don't let
all that you
don't know about me
scare you away
from taking the dive...
        I am as close to God as
        human capacity can reach.
I am a favorite
creation of the Creator,
an unspoken
wonder (wander) of the world.
It does you no service
to push away
your magnetic pull
towards me.
        Let go and fall in deep.
You'll begin to notice
the more you release,
the more healing you'll bring
and soon
muscle memory
will freely flow you
to fulfillment and enjoyment...
To give is to make
the space to receive;
I'll swim to you
if you'll paddle towards me
and once we
meet in the middle
you'll finally see
you, too
are a creation of the ocean...

Sometimes you wail
with your arms towards the sky;
**it'll be 11:11**
**and you'll be making wishes**
**that future generations will thank you for,**
or maybe that you'll regret
but never forget
that the human experience
was meant to make you feel something
-and all of it-
Even the parts that leave you
wailing towards the sky
with outstretched hands,
praying for a miracle...

You might just get it

or maybe you won't
(this time)

but there are
countless more miracles
waiting on you
to meet them there...

Just make it through this moment
and maybe a few more tough ones after that-

Your resilience
lays the steppingstones
to your clear
and concrete
path.

Keep going.

**I am in my season of rain,**
patiently accepting nourishment
while the fruits of my labor
fertilize and solidify.

You cannot expect seeds
to produce harvest
so quickly
after being planted.

Prepare your table for increase.

Clear dirty dishes
and create room for the feast
that awaits you.

Pull up a couple more chairs,
you'll have company accompanying...

Get out your silver spoons.

Come hungry.

**I learned to take
the love that I am given
with a grain of salt.**

It is hard to break deep
when you're meeting
a woman of the ocean.

I have a lot of fresh scars
that ache
when the rain pours,
**but at least I know**
**I survived**
**what was trying**
**to wound me.**

**I have wept
and cleansed my soul of darkness.**

I have wept
and gained clarity
from washed eyes.

I have wept
and watched clouds disperse
from the storm internal.

Let your tears act as soul food,
like fresh rain to a sunflower.

These are the grounds that blooms gardens.

This is the land
that cannot be shaken;
no matter how hard the earth quakes,
no matter how far people separate,
that won't burn when ember touch it...

There is power in the cleanse,
in the pour,
in the pain.

And there's beauty in
wiping clean
a slate
for another day.

**I healed dying petals
with tears of love**
and watered the root of the problem.
And the flower grew
right through the roof,
without release she wouldn't have solved it.

**Green-eyed girl with the speckled face,
you can tell a story with a closed mouth...**

Life has poured itself into you
and brought every ounce of self-knowing to surface.

And here you drip...

Leaving puddles of understanding and evolution
in every space you inhabit.

You have learned the importance of weathering every storm.

If there were ever a man
strong enough to brace himself
in the depth of your ocean,
you would swallow him
in change of current.

How often do we praise a Riptide?

Reliable in source,
you do not project what you are not,
inside.
A storm,
a tidal wave,
a rainy day
and holy water...
You are a reflection of both cleansing and drowning.

Water girl.

With the green eyes and speckled face...
If only you were not grounded by earth, today.

**EMBRACE.**
Understand the purpose of every flaw
and what it's here to show you...
Where you so blindly
mistreat yourself from lack of time
and give more care
to those who face you
than to the face that belongs to you...

**LOVE.**
For every feature that reminds you of origin...
In messy brows
and lashes that whisper
until given voice
to speak their truth...
This person belongs to (is the product of) many lifetimes.

**RENEW.**
Strip away any remnants of masks or coverage of character...
For peace to settle in,
it starts with removal
of anything with an overserved purpose.
Everything that you are
is everything you are supposed to be...

**Now GROW.**
You have been watered and fed.
Lay harvest in untouched fields
and mend the garden of your heart...

Watch yourself
as you bloom with grace.

**Throughout the week,
I felt like blue.**
From little reminders,
small tiffs
and missing you...
And then I remembered,
the blue can wash clean
from waves
and summer rain,
I'm immersed
and set free...
I'm one with the colors,
and they give me life too.
So this week,
just this week,
I've adopted
the color "blue."

I must go
as deep for myself
as the depths
I've submerged myself in
for the likeliness of others.

**I must be able
to stand the pressure
of being alone
with myself.**

If there were ever a time
you felt so low
you could meet your shadows
at the base of their feet,
I would remind you
of how seeds are buried in dirt
and rise with care,
but they cannot sprout
without first being planted...

Maybe you feel so low
because your ceiling is higher
than the standards you set for yourself
and you are aware
of the space
that awaits your alignment.

Find clarity in moments of faith...
When you don't quite know
what you will become,
but you will undoubtedly
grow.

**Be rooted, but flow.**

**Soul-training**
comes in waves of destruction,
looking forward
to your reaction...

You will be tested
over the things
that you pray for.

How you handle adversity
determines the level
of your blessing.

**Today is a day
is a day
is a day...**

We've been here before
with misty eyes,

but as rain has cleared our vision,
we understand
not every day
calls for sun...

I sit quietly
waiting for the sight of blooming flowers,
internal and external.

As seasons shift,
each day is faced
with its own forecast.

Regardless,
we are evolving towards warmth.

As we grow and our layers shed,
bare skin calls for
vulnerability.

I often lay naked in preparation,
shouting truth
and waiting for it
to echo back to me.

...

Glimpses of light
peeks through overcast skies.

A momentary sun-sighting
will fuel you enough
to hold you until summer.

Remember the lessons the cold taught you,
but understand
the frigid is not all there is to see...

Accept your hibernation,
respect your need for rest.

**It is almost time for you to stand tall,
sweet sunflower.**

**If my heart were a place
it'd look like
your favorite getaway island-**

Surrounded by crystal-clear water
in an abysmal ocean,
my hydration is transparent.
Take advantage
of its nourishment...
The island creatures
don't mean any harm.
They'll only attack when provoked.
They take protection very seriously,
after all,
this is their home.
Fruit falls freely
from the forest trees-
The most ripe and juicy you'll find,
I promise you that.

Another subtle reminder
to feed your soul.

Take an extra bite if you must...

The trees all stand their ground;
unfaltering,
their roots run deep.

They sing silent hymns
that resonate loudly,
giving life
with every exhale.
They breed a deep peace,
starting inward,
extending outwards-
Even their branches
welcome you with open arms...

...

Life is remote,
there's footprints in the mud
of past travelers-

There's far and few,
but they were here nonetheless...

Some of them brought gifts
or planted seeds,
while others trampled
on fresh harvest...

You'll be impressed
by the island's
self-restoration...

It depends on time for healing.

If you stay too long
you might go mad,
not everyone can handle
so much life,
content in its place.

Most of us
are addicted to the chaos
so the visits are often short-
leaving feelings
of nostalgia;
your visit will be a
memory of a lifetime.

It's likely you'll reminisce forever...

This is your reminder to take a breath.

This is your reminder that it's ok to take a break.

This is your reminder that yes,
there are 1 million things to do
and yes,
it feels like there isn't enough time,
but there is a reason
we have a limited amount of hours
in every day.

**This is your reminder to be a human.**

This is your reminder to check in on your mental and emotional state.

This is your reminder to cleanse.

This is your reminder that self-renewal is crucial.


Love,
a water baby.

# EBB & FLOW

**One with the sun,
intuitive love,
you shift gracefully with the seasons.**

To and fro
your heart still goes
attaching and then releasing.

You haven't mastered the craft
of ultimate give-back
the time which you have wasted.

Just towards yourself
the moments, they've felt
distracted and romantic...

We make it seem,
these "little" things
like something may not matter-

But time adds up
and then it's cut,
what else then are you left with?

I like to feel,
it makes me real,
reminds me I'm still human.

But deep inside,
my spirit rides
she's ready for enhancement...

Towards the sky I go...

I've realized
pain isn't useless,
it's reminded me
where to grow;
and though sometimes
I have felt helpless,
it's important that we know
the world won't stop
and life won't quit
begging you
to learn balance.
So even when
you're at your "lowest"
you still know
how high
your climb is...
We've been on top,
we've feared the drop
but gained
that we'd survive it.
So now it's time,
we can't rewind
we must
push forward
out of darkness...

**The sun still exists behind the clouds,
however timely in appearance.**

I'm on the search for freedom,
who it is
or what it means...
Because although
I have no shackles,
I still feel them
subconsciously.
With every move
we say or do
we're watched or listened-in.
And so it seems
the closest freedom
is observing changing winds-
It comes and goes
a whisper or flow
invisible when it breathes.
And sometimes
-oh just sometimes-
I feel jealous of the breeze.
Although I cannot see you,
you're reminder that life moves.
And no matter if
you're ready or not,
you still are moving too.
These days,
time moves in circles,
and you'll surely be here again.
Just take some time
for present moments
so the circle
can start again.

**Every day is a new beginning.**

**Nostalgia is a thief**
of all the beliefs
I solidified.

It goes back in time
and replaces
periods with commas
whispering "what if's"
where "not even's" should be.

I know my truth,
but sometimes it feels good
to bend a little.

Maybe there's better ways
to exercise my imagination
than to replay the same story
and wish for a better outcome
this time around.

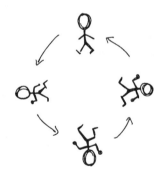

Sometimes I reminisce
on the "could have's" and "what if's..."

I think about the life we had,
the soul connection
with a clouded past...

I wonder if the times had changed,
would our love
still have strayed away?

But faith is truth,
and sometimes
mistakenly fuels lies;

and with that
we were bound to meet
the fate of our love's demise.

I'm thankful for the time we had
although the ending
drives me mad...

Today I wouldn't change a thing,
because now my voice is back
and my heart
will relearn to sing...

**Thank you for the heartbreak;
thank me for the rebuild.**

**We were born into a fucked-up generation
of being instantly aware of trauma-**
Came out of the womb addicted...
Conflicted.
We are always afraid that we're always dying.
And we are...
Slipping away too early haunts me.
I am the Queen of rebuked thoughts.
Am I cancelling manifestations
or silencing my intuition?
Either way I don't want it...
In a perfect world
I'd live forever
and be ridded of these manic thoughts.
Everything comes and goes,
sort of like my memories.
Moments turn into them
after you blink.
We're made to think
that sleep is for the weak.
If you're depressed
you need deep rest,
thank Jim Carrey for that.
Life in color
leaves less room
for faded lines.
Everyone makes you feel
like you have to pick sides.
Vulnerability is a loaded gun
pointed north.
Forgive yourself,
engage your wealth,
work harder than you want to...
Life's a long list
of up next's and to-do's.

**Tonight I sat in grief
with my vessel...**
Warm tears grazed against
flushed cheeks
in this vessel.
I truly haven't been enough for you.
When I sit in silence,
the psilocybin
reminds me of my truth...
There's nothing more important
than tending to my roots.
I'm so sorry
for what I've done to you.
Body folded over my hands and knees,
I pray to live another day.
Sometimes I beg for God
to take it all away-
The thoughts that consume
in a darkened room,
the ones that tell me
I'm close to my doom...

I don't wanna slip from this vessel.

Sometimes I feel I'm losing my grip
in this vessel.

And I don't wanna spend another day
without acknowledging
it's a treasure-
because not everyone
gets another day to breathe
in their vessel...

Thank you for unconditional resilience...
I love you / I'm sorry / Forgive me

Really,
**we're just
addicted to
taking deep breaths
and
filling empty spaces.**

I never had the type of love I needed for myself
until I had to get it alone.
I have been surrounded by wildflowers,
gardens,
trees of life
and burning bushes...

I recognized passion in others,
both for themselves
and for me...

But no flower ever helped me blossom
just by blooming on their own.

It took my own self-care;
my thirst for water as emotion
and hunger for sun as wisdom...
It took drying out and wilting
to understand
how much work I needed to do
to stand tall and poised.

On rainy days
I feel myself drowning
and sometimes the sun
sucks me dry...
But with the ebb and flow of life,
I am able to remain rooted
even in muddy soil.
I understand how to change with the seasons
and the importance of
losing leaves
to grow back new ones.

**Fall, to flourish...**

I forgot this part about recovery...

**Growing pains
still lead to growing
no matter how much
it hurts.**

Stand tall.
Fix your posture.
Deep breath.
Inhale.
Engage.
Deep breath.
Cry out.
Long stretch.
Deep breath.
2 steps.
1 more.
Deep breath.
You're home.
Deep breath.
Relax.
Relax.
Relax.

I'm so far behind
on a challenge that I made.

It's always at the end
that the race drives you insane.

You set a certain goal
that you really want to hit.

But in comes all distractions
and the rest just goes to shit.

But now I'm back on track
and I'll make up for my time.

Cuz at the end of the day
**it's so important**
**to finish what is mine.**

**Now it's time
to get back on track,**

to get the weight of distraction
right off of my back.

I want the sun
to spread light through me;

the darkness of the tunnel
will brighten
and I'll see

a love,
success,
and happiness too...

I'll re-meet my ambition
and run it brand new.

So now that it's time
to get back on track
you must be sure to remember
that even after loss,
there's nothing you lack.

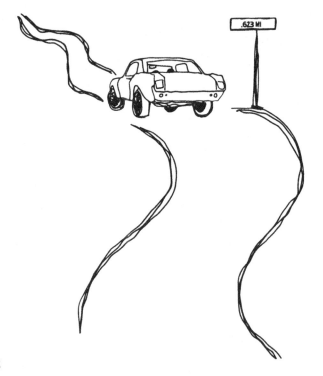

## An Ode to Tom Misch, Mulholland Drive & my Past Lover

In the midst of it all,
all I wanted
was for you to come back home.
Your love was a beautiful escape;
painted with colours of freedom,
radiating warmth like sunshine.
What if we started over?
We could wake up this day
and take on a journey
that required nothing but
tightly-held hands and loosened hearts...
Unbound by the memory of the present.
Wander with me...
With you,
we're so close
but create friction with
over-active minds and under-active souls...
The reverie of yesterday
was jaded by paper planes
traveling towards tomorrow.
And I just want to release with You.
I rub across your skin in the dark,
keeping me warm and safe
like nightgowns to a growing girl...
Hark.
For the answers deemed necessary
to save this love
is an intensified one.
When you're aligned to love,
the feeling of pride requires destruction
and I am learning
to crumble for you...
We are not ephemeral, but eternal.
And with that,
we must follow the one who is...
In love,
in light,
to create your own.

**I am strong,
but I am triggering.**

My essence alone
brings out overthought voices
reaching to speak louder
than the tone
my energy brings...

I am a mirror.

It's up to the person
looking inside of it
to determine
whether beauty or despair
leaks out the cracks
in the reflection.

I come looking
like I'm asking
to be apart of your world
and the heaviness it brings...

I show you that you need to be heard
and it often gets yelled back to me.

I understand,
but not enough
to fall down to your depths
with ease.

Life is challenging,
but you'll survive
if you just breathe...

**Sometimes you're the hurricane
and other times
you're the clear blue sky
above gentle ocean waves...**

Our minds are storms
but we know the importance
of holding our winds
and watering the crops around us.

We were sent to uplift and uphold,
not dig up and destroy.
Mother Nature
took her time with us
and whispered songs
of changing seasons
that sang loud
in a heavy winter breeze.

Not everyone can handle the cold.

We were like the trees of pine,
wise in our years with wide eyes.
Our love was oxygen
and we worked overtime
to fuel our environments
throughout transition.

Now the importance lies
in exchanging faith as our tithe
and moving forwards
towards purpose
with punctuality.

May we be the example
of how a single sapling
spreads seed by release
and expands territory
which welcomes
new healing.

**The declaration moment**

Today is the mark
of a brand new journey
with myself.
I have officially been tossed
head-first
into the ring with the devil
and I almost let him win.
I know in this moment,
I am exactly where
I'm supposed to be.
The sleepless nights,
worry-filled days,
anxiety-driven thoughts and actions
and numerous times
of what felt like
screaming under water
have all lead me here...
Home.
To lay a steady ground
before I begin my rebuild.
I hear you, God.
I am abiding by the steps
You are ordering for me...
I've been ignoring You.
I thought my way was the right one...
As if I forgot
You have created All,
including my path,
which has already been paved
for me, by you.
I would be lying if I said
oblivion was not
still taunting me,
even after my awakening.

...

I sit here
battling the guilt
for being asleep so long
in the first place...
I've missed so much.
I've been aimlessly walking forward
with a blindfold on,
not realizing
the power my two hands have
to remove all
that disables me.
This is a journey
of deep de-rooting
and re-planting.
Finding the termites in the soil,
removing them
and sowing myself
back on fertile ground.
God move my spirit
closer to you.
Give me a Home
in a space I can
feel
hear
see
breathe- You.
You have made it clear
I will self-destruct
without you.

**-Flying now**
**Taking off towards re-discovery...**
Not a "goodbye"
Just a see Me later.

All that time
I wanted to die

I never realized

I was just trying
to put an end

to the self
that wasn't me...

**Suicide to my old self.**








Heaven's on the ground now.

**[ Read me like a breath; Inhale. Exhale.]**

The part that felt like magic
no longer exists.

You trigger parts of me
that no longer desire to be awakened.

When you stand in front of me
it blocks me from being able to see myself.

Sometimes
God gives you exactly what you wish for.

Sometimes
you would've done better off without it.


Maybe one day
it'll all make sense.

And maybe that day
we can meet again.


**~A releasing of toxic air**

[breathing exercises]

# THE PROCESS (of You)

Maybe
it's not that
I know you better
than you know yourself;
maybe it's that
I know your
better self
better than
you know,
yourself...

The self that has been
discouraged from acknowledging
the light at the end of the tunnel
because it's distracted
by the length of the tunnel,
itself.

The self that is
waiting for you
to catch up to it.

The self that
gracefully reigns in peace
and is abundantly prosperous
off of thoughts,
alone.

**That's the you**
**I see...**
**That's the you**
**I know,**
**even when you don't...**

In this next month,
between this full moon and the next
I will continue learning to soften my grip...
**I'm beginning to grow overly accustomed
to the things my heart yearns for,**
forgetting attachment does not equal out to love
even though I have plenty of that, too.
May I love harder and shout my gratitude towards the sky,
breaking back open my voice
that has been keeping itself tucked away
inside a crooked rib cage,
deceiving my thoughts of protection.
Sometimes our overcautiousness
leaves us unprepared
for adversity and adventure.
We play out scenarios
and rely on our expectations so much
that once it gets thrown off track,
you feel like a part of your reality
has been taken away from you
(because it has)
How much time have we spent
living in our heads
that we waste
current seconds on expired moments?
My presence must be present.
My patience must beam brighter.
My voice must heave louder.
My heart, opened bigger.
I pray my problem solving gets the better of me;
to unlock creativity
in the left side of my treasure chest,
with ideas flowing like a river's creek
after a heavy week of rain...
Take note of the way
it empties itself into
bigger beds for holding...
Evolution will always be a journey
of our ability
to balance phases and fullness
as they coexist on their own.

I've been
putting off
time for myself
waiting on
time to move
in forward motion
even though
it never stops
for anyone
even when
you're feeling stuck
everything else
continues on
with
or without you.
Tomorrow
like today
was never promised
but here we are
and there you go,
you mustn't quit
just look within
or you'll fall out
**it's time for you**
**to make time**
**for yourself.**

We've all gone a little mad,
I let distractions
eat my soul.
I've turned
into another creature
who embraces
the unknown.
She might laugh
a bit too much
but the fun times
never end;
**I used to
be scared of my shadows
now they've become my best friends...**

Welcome to the Palace.

Inspired by "The Shadow of the Palace" collaboration with Mimi Haddon

**Be mindful with your words,
they are spells.**
Be courageous enough
to speak what you need
and what you know
in the present moment
it calls for...
There is no need to delay
what was so promptly
discovered by you...
Sometimes broken promises
feel like a plucking of petals.
Although we understand
expectation is of our own
self-administered torture,
there are still barriers of safety
that a good action
followed by a good word
can build and provide.
It is in your own best interest
to be a leader of the movement...
A way-maker for healing
through our own awareness.
And what a beautiful world
that would be...
Strength, strengthened by strength.

We are walking swords
with bulldozers
strapped to our feet...

**My human experience is meant to be just that,**
to learn, to love, to grow, to die...
To come back and begin again.
This vessel is a routine.
We are unaware of expiration dates
but it rings loud that they exist.
We do everything to prevent them
but in the end
it's time that wins...
Make every day count just like your last
because it might just be...

So what are you doing (today)
to be proud of yourself,
in case it's time to leave?

Spring.

The universal time for
"out with the old and in the with new,"
but what happens when
your cleaning
reminds you of
everything you once knew?

Old photographs and memories
of simpler times and a clearer head;
moving towards the future,
no danger
and nothing left unsaid...

But now that it's over,
it's time to dispose
of what no longer serves us;

thinking over and over
about who really fills our cups...

I was bound to replace
all the memories of you
with new places,
new faces
and all things fresh and renewed.

Life made me a lesson
and changed my view,
to prepare for the things
that were more aligned
with my truth.

**-Harmonious Spring Cleaning**

**And every day
she would rise like the sun-**
because it was her duty;
to share her light
whether (weather) foggy, cloudy or clear
She was always there...

But how often do we thank the sun for rising?

We thank the moon
and appreciate the stars...

but the Sun...

But the sun is too bright to look at...
Or too hot for us to bask in...
And even though
the sun gives us the longest love
-grasping on to the edge of the earth to wish us goodnight-
we give more endearment
to the sets and the rises
than the one responsible for the sight.

Our daily reminder
of luminous opportunity...

So she will continue rising like the sun,
regardless of praise,
because without it
the world would be a darker place...

To be the best leader
is to be
the most experienced follower.

How can you know
how to be a sergeant
if you don't know how
you like to be lead;
what works for a team
and the trials and tribulations
of being a soldier?

There's wisdom that comes
with protecting a pack.
There's lessons in
shedding blood in the field.
And you must learn the ropes of the terrain
to be strong enough to carry
the lives of other fighters
on your back...

A leader is gentle,
kind,
empathetic,
but firm.
Though you can mend and mold
you cannot break.

**So to be a leader**
**is to be a follower-**
**with the highest regard,**
**for a life that is bigger**
**than all of ours.**

There are people I had placed
on a pedestal
that had me placed
on their dusty corner shelf.

I mistook the fact
that I had a "place"
and convinced myself
I was something more meaningful
than the trinket
they loved to keep
but never made use
or shined light on.

A simple convenience for rare occurrences...

If they want you,
they will take you with them
and show off
wherever they go.

**I am more than a moment
to take up space with.**

Your seat on the pedestal
has been replaced
with my own.

If I find you
over-indulging in my presence,
enough to make you
forget how
one-of-a-kind it is,
it is now my responsibility
to bring you back to Earth
through an over-indulgence
of my absence.
I know better than to give
any one-person
the power
to change my own perspective
on the gift that is
myself.
There are others who
unwrap me consistently
but still act surprised
as if they've
received me for the first time.

Those are the people
whose hands
I long to rest in...
You can find me there
when you miss me.

**I won't be far,
but you can
feel me from a distance.**

**I have lived this past year with a blindfold on,**
peeking through the bottom to see
what is happening in front of me...

My only goal was to keep moving.
To see "enough" to where I wouldn't trip,
"enough" to take the next step,
but not "enough" to tell you where I've been.

Veiled and disconnected...

There was something about this thing around my eyes
that acted as a blanket
rather than a block.

I never saw it for what is was,
because it kept me warm
from what I thought was cold
in exterior.
But when I finally took it off,
I was able to see the cold for what it really was...

Me.
A sheep in lion's clothing,
all I wanted was to be herd,
but the roar was what I was used to.

The strong one...
The one who has it all,
knows it all,
fights for it all...
I was lacking guidance.

I ignored my shepherd and spent a year in the jungle.
I hunted food that wasn't for me,
found shelter in foreign homes
and prayed for the royalty of a lion
when I lacked obedience as the sheep.

...

**Identity crisis.**

Now here I am in new skin,
empty but hungry.

What you are seeing is a rebirth,
and there is no telling when
this body will feel like mine again...
But at least it is.
What more can one say
when everything has been said?

The lack of presence causes the most ache,
but we know this...

Two burnt-out souls,
perfectly matched
yearning again for the flame..
We had the type of love that could set forest fires;
explosive and warm,
but we cringe at the thought of destruction.

What if instead of a perfect match,
we could be a perfect whole
and appreciate ourselves in reflections of each other?

This isn't what I do it for,
but it seems to take a weight off.

Hope.
I just want you to be the best version of you,
as you do, me..

And I pray one day
we can experience all the best parts of ourselves
on our own,
together.

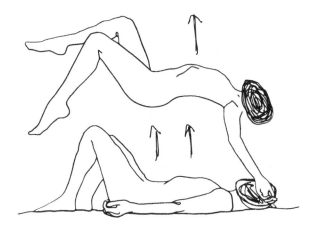

What if I told you,
that the only person
and the only thing
getting in your way
is you?

That those obstacles
were only meant
to test your strength,
not to stop you.

That the speed bumps are telling you
to *slow down,*
look around you
and enjoy the process.

That not every day will be good,
but at least you're learning...

You've already overcome your worst days
and you still haven't lived your best days.

But first,
you have to get out of your own way.

You have to accept what you cannot change
and change what cannot be accepted.

Nothing is in control,
except for you,
over you.

**It's time for you to live.**

**When everything around you is shaking,
be the firm foundation
in which nothing can crumble...**

Stand strong and tall in your love,
faith
and purpose.

Give an abundance of what you feel is lacking.

Receive what life gives you with open arms,
a strengthened mind
and a softened heart.

Be the person you so often look for,
today.

**As above, so below**
**I go with the flow**
in 10 hours' time
I've lifted afloat.

I studied the clouds
and thanked them for shade,
then with grace and patience
the sun said my name.

I whispered my worries,
She laughed loud, full faced.
"When you're surrounded by darkness,
still remember my place...

I never will leave you,
it's you that must go,
then relate the clouds to me,
As above,
So below."

Even on the gloomy days,
it is still possible to feel like sunshine.

Let your internal light shine on all those
who cross your path.

Radiate your warmth to someone who
needs a little extra...

Meditate away any clouds internal...
Find joy and magic in the ones in the sky.

**Weather your storm**
**and your rainbow will come...**

We must crack
We must break
We must peel
We must reveal

In order to find
the solid foundation
in which we need
to heal.

**- A remodeling of sorts.**

# CREATOR

**My mood's accustomed to the moon,**
when she stretches full
I come undone.
I can no longer
hold my breath or
keep my feelings
bundled up...

I overstand,
I hear lives loud
they often
ring back onto me;
the moon shines bright,
it casts out dark
and brings the light
everyone needs.
If in your soul
the night feels cold
the sun will
greet you
here shortly;
but hold on tight
embrace tonight
and new beginnings
after spring.

**-Flowers on the Moon**

**Lord take my hand
as I walk with You,
blindfolded for the months ahead...**

I'm throwing myself into deeper faith with You,
I don't trust what my eyes can see...

The human in me
distorts my truth
or claims a want as a need-
I can't afford to mold this way.

Discipline...
In myself,
to reach for You
instead of warm hands
for a Home.
I overstay my welcome this way...

Your hospitality is eternal.

Hold me back
when my tongue wants to run...
Remind me that there is a difference
between a prison
and rehabilitation center.

My jaws act as gates
but You give me permission
to come and go as I please...

I ask You give me peace
to remain inside
when chaos tempts me outwards.

Again,
discipline.

I know there is a blessing
in my favor
on the other side
of these challenges,
accomplished with a strong heart
and a strong faith
in God.

**The air is always thinner
at the top of the mountain
but yet
the view is what ends up
taking your breath away.**

**I'm grateful to wake up today**
and every day
for this past
quarter of a century...
And with that,
the every day wake up
from myself
and the other
Quarter Century-ers
in my generation
has initiated
the wakeup of a lifetime
and hundreds of years
worth of lifetimes
in the earth
and all the humans
who inhabit it around us.
We are a generation
starving for growth,
impact and change.
We wear our hearts on our sleeves
to lead by love and example.
We are a walking Revolution.
We demand justice and peace
in the same breath.
We question everything
for learning and understanding
and-speak our truth
with intention
for the world to hear.
We are loud, proud and in charge...
So I'm grateful to wake up today
and every day
because I know
we're all waking up together,
and I know
every day we wake up

...

is a day
someone else
feels loved and seen
for the first time from our well-doing.
And while I celebrate today
as the day
I came into the world,
I also feel the need
to celebrate
all of those
so divinely-timed
to come into the world
and give it life,
accompanying each other
in the biggest shift of consciousness
the world has ever seen.
Happy Soul Day to us all.
**We are all connected.**
**I feel us running deep today...**

25.
6/23

Sometimes
it feels good
to pretend
that I am
the only person
who matters...

But most times,
I see myself
inside
the beings of others...

And then I remember
what it feels like
to be
just like them
too.

There is hardly a difference
between me
and then you...

**We are
stars
inside skin.**

I love the diversity in clouds...
No two look the same
and they're constant shape-shifters.
They never reach a final form
and they're celebrated
for their ability in adaptability.
The most vulnerable earth-creation of all;
they raise themselves high,
full of oxygen and tears
to stand firm in form,
but ready to shift as the wind calls for...
They're guided by faith,
wherever nudged, they follow.
They're not afraid to stand alone
and still know
when to follow the crowd.
At chance,
they give opportunity
to see through to brighter sky,
they trust in others' time to shine...
They don't intend to block us from the light,
but protect from overheating.
They understand the power of warmth
but the dangers of a burn.
Soft and gentle,
but robust and proud...
**I think we could all live a little more
like the clouds.**

**God has been waking me up
on His own time-**
bright and early
when my mind holds
open spaces
like a bright-green field,
untouched
and hungry for possibility.
He looks for the time
when nobody's voice
but His own
can make its way
inside my ears
and towards my soul...
When concernment in questions
can immediately be answered by
a multitude of solutions
to sort through
and weigh out...
He knows He has
alone time to catch back up on
and has wasted
no time
bringing it to
the center of my attention.
Keep waking me up, God.
Or keep me up
as late
or as early
as you need
to reach me.
I'm all ears,
wide-eyed and open-souled.
Your plan for my life
is all I long to know.

**How come when it's time
to buckle down and dial in,
it all feels so easy to throw away?**
Like the many moments
on well-practiced discipline
and hours of daydreams about the future
could never really happen to you?
Why do we put a halt in the flow
when we're so steadily
on our way
to bringing the cinematic life
we see in our heads
to reality?
Interrupt and dig down deep...
When did you so easily
allow yourself to lose sight
of the rope that led you
through the murky insights
of your mind?
When did the fear
of the depth of the ocean
distract you
from the creations
that exists within it?
Though life is full of uncertainty,
it is also full of adventure.
We gain our wisdom by experience
and we cannot know about
what we have not gone about...
Do not let the brightness of the future
blind you from shining your own light.
Put a spotlight on what holds you back.
Ignite a fire in the motion of what moves you forward.

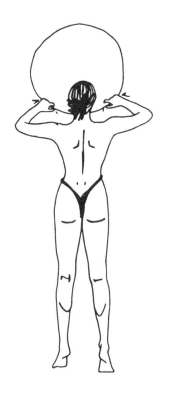

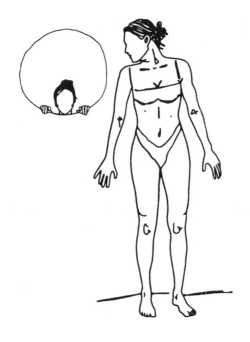

How come sometimes when God speaks
we make the choice
to face the other way?

Like the words would just
bounce off our backs
like we aren't
already used to
storing all our energy there...

Everything sticks.

Whether wisdom stands
in the forefront of your cranium
or lies dormant until awakened,
**you cannot escape**
**what is destined**
**to transition you.**

There can be no peace
until you simply
surrender.

Although we are filled with fire,
it still
is unnecessary to burn.


May your light lead the way...

**On this day, I pray for peace**
in your heart,
in your mind
and through
the people
that you see.

Though you cannot fill the void
of what is gone
or what's been lost,
now you have beings of light
who will protect you
at all costs...

It's been a tough year,
our faith & strength ultimately tested,
but above anything else
we still chose love to invest in...

It might get a lot worse,
-or maybe better-
from here;
but in the end,
all that we know
is to hold our loved ones near.

I don't know what's coming next,
something big or unexpected...
So I pray it's for the best
and we'll feel much more connected.

So on this day,
I pray for peace-
and that you receive love
at least, you'll have it here, from me...

I take advantage of the sunshine
and the way it hits my face,
like the ray's a familiar lover
and it warms my soul with grace.
I never question its position
when too hot or behind clouds
because the sun it does its job,
always
day in & then day out...
We expect so much from the Sun
to provide and then to leave
but we don't give enough
appreciation
to the one who makes sure we see-
all the beauty in a day
and then its' Sister Flames
at night...
So today, I'll remind the sun
that its love
is a delight.

**The light of the world,**
**what a beautiful sight...**

**D**ivine in the knowledge of her own greatness,
she has a fire burning deep within
that has no desire
of ever being extinguished.
**R**eaching to be better, than herself, day after day...
She is in competition with no one
but her own growth.
**E**nlightened in love,
she understands there is no greater power
then the magic of what a happy, giving heart can do.
**A**micable to growth, she welcomes creativity with open arms
and views the world with a fish-eye lens...
Open minded, and ready for exploration.
**M**ighty, influential and inspirational.
There are eyes that will not see clearly
until they find her.
**E**thereal in the way she moves...
Like she's been here in past lifetimes,
with wisdom like a giving tree.
**R**esilient in her firm foundation.
Resourceful in the present moment...
**S**he is armed for battle with love as her weapon.
May she understand the importance of killing with kindness.

[ Dedicated to Asia and Kimora Dreamer ]

**I awaken with the mood of the sky.**
We understand each other best that way,
how it quietly announces
its intentions for the day...
A gentle breeze,
a hint of sun
and a misty dew
reminds us that all life
cleanses during rest time.

Today she greets me
with a warm horizon,
and that's the mood
I'm adopting to stay...

Good morning, morning.

Thank you for the light today.

**In summer sun,
I'm gently kissed
by the rays of bright love
across my skin...**

And though too long
would do me wrong,
no tone of skin
makes the love less strong...

There's something about
the beach and sand
that attracts all souls
to rejoice in this land.

And even though the time's passed
of "hello's" and head-nods,
the way the water greets the sand
makes up
for the time that's been lost.

I hope if I create life,
that they get to see
all the beauty I've experienced
and then appreciate it
more than me...
But for now I feel
deeply grateful and blessed
for this day to reflect
and this day for sun-rest.


-A day at the beach

**Nothing I crave
is physical.**

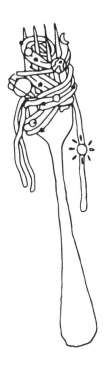

Think a little bigger baby...
If you broaden your mind,
you just might find
your soul on the horizon.

**Your spirit guides
want to tell you the world,**
but first you must
give yourself
permission to listen.

# LOVE LANGUAGE

**It's easier for me
to push away**
than it is
for me
to stand with open arms.

I am used to runners
and mouths that
think words are actions,
or can't wrap minds around
putting effort towards
kindness of the tongue.

Figure out
which love language
plays a part
in every relationship
you're in.

Be an equal
-and mindful-
opponent of the game.

Companionship
built off
hunger for company
will burn out the spark
before it even
has the chance
to become a flame...

Explosive passion
is the cause
for quick destruction.

Tread lightly,
pace slowly.

**Do not rush the process
of a forever thing.**

I know that I'm good
of taking place after place
of the girl that you meet
before you settle in your space.

I teach a man how to love
show him how good that it feels
to be loved by a woman
who gives him something real.

If you talk about dreams,
I'll reach for yours too.
Give you tips and good tricks
and support what you do.

But I know that it's rare
to find someone like me,
and although it may take longer,
one day someone will see.

**If you love me real hard,**
**I'll return it back to you**
**but as a love for yourself**
**when I love myself, too.**

I was committed to protect
this heart of stone.
I couldn't shake the thought
of it finding
a new home.

I'm turning soft,
from boulder to gravel,
I felt a kiss on the cheek
and began to unravel.

**Love, you changed me...**

**Love
is a fight.**

Love
is a commitment
towards the bettering
of other people
and yourself
simultaneously
all at once.

Love
is having both
a partner in crime
and partner in defense...

You are a soldier
for your partner
in love.

You are a best friend,
a safe space,
a healer,
a hand-crafted mirror...

And if you don't find yourself fit
don't settle
for a love
that doesn't reflect
the goodness
you already have stored
inside.

**In the mornings I miss
skin to skin contact
and butterfly kisses
that reign from eyes to stomach.**

I miss the smell of your Home,
my favorite neighbor
opening our blinds
at the same time
to mouth "good morning,"
but quietly...

Gentle enough not to wake the birds.

We spent the most time here...
Wrapped in love that kept us warm
like comforters in winter.
You made me excited to wake up
and every day was like Christmas,
hoping you'd unwrap me...

Or maybe we could just spend
a little quality time
in each other's presence...
All the things I long for
makes nighttime feel darker
and I don't want to close my eyes
because I know
I won't wake up next to you.

**I'd rather stay awake looking at the moon,
wondering if you remember
the promises
you made to her too...**

**I forgot what intimacy felt like...**

I forgot that for a man
to truly know me,
see me naked,
he must caress me first
from the inside-out.

Soul-stimulation.
Does he penetrate my mind
and keep my heart on beat?

I know I'm home
when it doesn't skip.

I like it when you hold me there.

Peel open my layers of vulnerability...
Penetrate my mind
and rock my heart
on beat...

I know I'm coming home
when it doesn't skip.

Warm.

I forgot what intimacy felt like...
I forgot that to truly see me,
naked,
You must wish to caress me
from the inside-out...

I forgot what intimacy felt like,
but I'll bet that you'll remind me.

**He is the sun eternally;**
I bloom,
his flower
for earth to see.
But in the scheme of us,
Universally
I remain the moon,
he reflects light in me.

**I've always envied the cup
of his morning coffee...**

The first thing to grace his lips
before a day
of saving the world with them.

I'm eager to
spend the most holy time
of the new day
with you.

When God is planting little seeds
in your garden
that are waiting to bloom
unto others.

I admire you right in His precious light,
surrounded by Palm Trees
and slight buzzing from the outside world.

My love longs for you in the morning time...

I found my twin flame
with flowers in his eyes,
passion bursting from his mind,
that enflamed all of mine...
I kept his soul close to me.
The warmth of his fire
was a sight to see.
He burned blindingly bright,
eternally.
I knew I found my match.
Without second guessing
I fell and I latched,
yet detached...
We spent a lifetime playing catch
up.
In every dimension
the tension developed.
How far can you run from a soul tie?
No matter length we go,
the feeling multiplies-
like you were made to fit perfectly
by my side
and I don't want this feeling
to subside.
You light me up like dynamite.
A soul explosion of colors
filled the sky.
The stars remind me of your love
tonight.
They kiss my forehead
as sleep fills my eyes.
I hope you feel
my soul in flight...
If you're awake,
I'll meet you deep
under the moonlight.

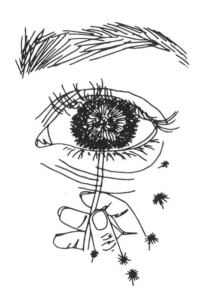

**I've been smoking on the tail-ends
of the joints you left behind.**
I figure,
if I save a drag-a-day
maybe the taste of your lips
won't fade away...
There's still an imprint
where your fingers
tightly gripped
before you pulled in
to take the hit.
I reach for my nape
simultaneous to
the deep inhale of
tightly-packed collard greens.
I close my eyes
so I can see yours.
You fill up soccer fields
with dandelions and sunshine...
God always gets a
kick out of you,
knowing you're prone
to kick it right back.
With an exhale,
my oxygen escapes
the same way
you take my breath away.
Tongue-tied to the trip of tailored talents...
I learned all of yours
fit perfectly with mine.
I could be entertained
just by the idea of you
forever...
I am grateful you exist
without fiction.
Your energy alone
releases lifetimes of karmic pleasures.

**You gave me the gift
of warm Sake on my lips...**
You governed
the opportunity
to taste the love
that I give
so frequently...
Intoxicating.
You fill me with life,
mindfully.
You heat the core
of my soul
effortlessly.
Now here I am,
repeatedly licking my lips
to feel the way
yours grazed
across my skin...
Your soul
left a piece of itself
with me...

Thank you.

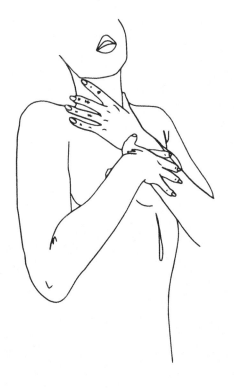

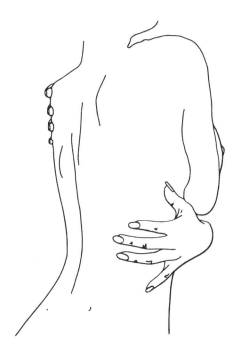

**I guess since you're not here**
**I'll have to just**
**replace your hands with my own...**

Wrap my fingers around my throat
and imagine how it feels
to be at the tips
of your hard work...
Strength seeps from your fingers
and into my soul.

I can teleport to the time
you spent getting yourself
to where you are now,
simply from your energy...

My back arches
to move closer
to be touched
by the thought of you.

Held gently, rubbed firmly...
It's a pleasure to me
to be studied by you.

Your tongue, my favorite magnifying glass.
Paying close attention to detail,
you don't miss a thing.

Every move you make
leaves me wishing
I could replay a moment
a million times over
just to experience it again...

Every touch somehow still feels like the first.

Your eyes answer prayers for me.

...

Our breath synchronizes as we realize
depth is important in muscle memory.

As you scale my body, I scale your thoughts in harmony...

I know where you're headed,
but I have patience in the journey.

If anything, it's my favorite part.

Your sun greets my petals with familiarity...
Your warmth feeds my soul
and I can't help but open up to you.

I long for this greeting,
this embrace,
this reunion.

You feel like home-base to a nomad,
the only thing,
I fantasize to return to.

My heart races
with every brush of your lips
on secure territory.

I'd give up all this land for you,
beg for you to settle down on it...

I've traveled many lifetimes
to be in this space with you,
and I'll travel many more
if it means
solidifying this bond in eternity...

**Your soul, it means the world to me.**

Sometimes I underestimate your strength.
I forget the traumas you've been through
that have built scar tissue
at the feet of your foundation.

I forget you have lived another lifetime than me...
Consciousness flowing before I was brewing.

You hide it all so well.

You mask your pain with silence,
thinking.
Lots of thoughts, carefully placed.

You move slower than me but with good intention...

Patience.

You take the chance to observe and grow...
A flower by association.
You bloomed through concrete in the dark,
a true miracle.

Thank you for planting yourself beside me...
I feel the oxygen you provide
just from being in the same vicinity.
A gift from the earth...

Naturally you provide without knowledge for why,
there's far and few like you.

And me,
**I'm sorry for the petals that I picked.**
**I got confused on which were wilting**
**and which needed more nourishment.**

...

**You become new with fresh water and strong soil
and I want to be the sun for you...**

Although you can never replace the roots you stemmed from,
you deserve to feel the warmth of a garden.

In times of remembering,
I feel deep pain for your losses.
I wish I could replace every memory
of empty pots
and vases too small.

I wish you would have had the opportunity
to grow up
with me...

But maybe that's why we're here now.

For me to share my seeds with you,
and for you to teach me
how to stand tall in the dark.

We grow together.

Unquestioning of the bases we were built from,
we enjoy each other's company.

Your leaves feel nice against mine...

And whether we're in the desert sun or drowning in the rain,
at least we'll have the opportunity
to bloom again and again.

His love was as deep as the ocean...
The waves at the end of his hair
curled me in like a riptide
and submerged me into
blue serenity...
He quenched my thirst.
He washed me clean.
From the mud he found a Lotus in me.
I entered his depths
like a block of concrete-
Ready to sink if he'd let me...
Through tidal and wave
the bits of rock gave
and broke me down
to soft pieces
of fertile ocean floor.
I was now home to a life that was bigger than me.
I was ground to firm roots which love grows on.
And now every time
the waves reach out to touch land,
He still makes sure
to hold on
tight to the sand...
**A love deep like the ocean**
**is all that you need**
**to learn the difference**
**from sinking or swimming**
**is just flowing...**

Thank you for being the root of the garden.
For being the firm ground for so many flowers to blossom on.

My wisdom tree

You are rooted, but you flow so smoothly.

A mantra I called my own and rediscovered through you.
I appreciate the way your branches give comfort
to all the birds who make a home in you.

They bear so much weight, but you never snap.

My wisdom tree

Shed your colors as the seasons change.
Allow yourself to bloom anew,
my love.
Dead leaves are useless to a growing tree.
Receive the oxygen you so freely release.

It's crazy how the earth
couldn't even survive
without someone like you...

**Do you even realize that you're
the wisdom tree?**

**You have given me
a newfound meaning of peace...**

A love that goes unsaid,
because action carries weight
where words falter.

When the outside world is your only worry,
but the safety of internal havens
hold you healed...

Moving through troubled water
seems lighter and easier.

Thank you for helping me tread
and keeping my head above water.

I don't need you to take my breath away,
when you are the source
that reminds me to breathe...


**(Oxygen)**

# GARDEN

**I found myself guarded
until you barged in**
holding the tools
for my garden
and how then
could my heart harden
for who could've been
the King
of love,
bargained.
You begged for time
to start again,
and here I am
under the stars' den
carefully connecting
to your jargon.
No matter where you go,
you'll never be
far again
cuz you hold the keys
to my garden,
now come in...

**In bare thoughts,**
**I was ready to let you read me...**
Skim each chapter
feel the roots of my words
lay firm to the seed of my soul...

Harvest.

They may try to pluck your petals,
withhold sun
or pour down rain-
But your roots can
withhold seasons
of growing love
or wilting pain.
Your colors
catch the eyes of those
who live with black and gray;
so when you feel
misunderstood
don't let your
vibrance fade away...
**Lift your chin
and face
the sun today.**

-Flower Girl

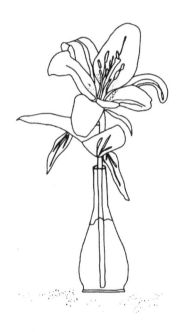

I never needed
to be accompanied
by bouquets,
**you found
the fullness in me
alone.**

Your favorite pick.

**I must believe in myself
to make this work,**
while taking hearts
in my hands
and planting seeds
in the dirt.
Don't wanna get your heart messy,
I'll dose it in water afterwards...
But still maybe
just -maybe-
you'll find seeds
wrapped up in yours...

And after a while
it'll sprout flowers,
grow a garden
under your shirt...
And to a greenskeeper,
it's a blessing
I didn't
over-tend
to make it work.

**I found peace in neutral colors,
they guided me back home**
to the ground that held a garden,
I was a Queen amongst the gnomes.
I sang with birds,
I played in dirt,
admired all my roots...
For the soil in which I'm planted
is rich in love,
it's loot.
Come find my treasure,
I promise not to
run before you leave.
I fall in fall,
full heart and all,
I branch out
with the trees.

**When I dance around naked,**
**I hear the trees call my name.**
They tell me to stretch my hands
and mirror the way they praise the sky.
They remind me
with crooked branches
that a wrangled spine
does not take away
what I was blessed to worship with.
My mindset changed...
I closed my eyes
and continued to move.
I felt the moon
radiating love
beyond my ceiling.
She rejoiced as my feet
gamboled the ground
to song.
When I hear my bones clap,
I imagine their applause.
To appreciate my body
from the inside out
is a new and improved
self-love.
I thank my skin for holding my limbs together.
I'm finding new ways
to honor this temple,
and gratitude serves
as a playground between
who I am
and who I'm yet to be...
Now here I am,
dancing naked in the dark,
connected to the sky by the knot on my head.
I wish the trees goodnight,
until we praise again...

**I long to be grazed
with soft fingertips
and solid intentions.**

I gave myself
permission to indulge
in anything that
bridges the gap
between my soul
and the outside world.

**Closed eyelids
look a lot like
flower petals,**
raining innocence
in their subconscious;
like a young child's attempt
at drawing the sun.

-Light flows through every eyelash-

Every day I'm reminded
of our connectedness to God;
with Oneness
and the undeniable ability
to go full circle...

After all,
that's the only thing
that's ever been consistent
anyway.

He used to be a darker soul,
closed off and enfolded
within himself.
He was drawn to red roses,
the way the petals stayed put
equally as confined as him.

Until one day from a crack in the window,
he felt the warmth of the sun
and stepped foot into light;
he was greeted by a sunflower
who changed his life,
and acted as a mirror
to see his own might
and began his own journey
towards blossoming.

He never knew
that all he needed
was to be
de-rooted & re-planted…
That the strength from the flower
stemmed from its ability
to face the sun & soak.
To simply BE-

**And this is how
the boy who thought he planted the wrong seeds
woke up to an entire garden.**
And never chased the darkness again.

Short and sweet,
your soul tastes like
honey to me…

And I am
always craving
another bite…

**-Human Honeycomb**

**I'm jealous of the planes in the sky,**
cuz I'm down here
and they know how it feels to fly.
With my head in the clouds
I'm free
and on my way to you...
And up here
there's no more turbulence
and the sky is blue
I feel your hue
it's translucent, too.
A film of love over every surface,
you tint everything in rainbows
and God knows
He distanced two
reluctant souls
who'll make it through...
But today I'm on the ground,
safe and sound,
with a deeper beating heart;
it feels the start
of newfound hope
and maybe
perfect works of art.
And when it's time
I'll get back up and
run right to the space of you–
He gave me
one big reason
in this season
to pay attention to:
the stillness that we need,
to thank the trees
and stretch our purpose through
none other than ourselves,
these bodies,

...

and the blessings
we don't think to use.
See when every day
it feels the same
we start to resent
the haze of gray
when really
all we needed
was some breath,
the sun and even
the downpours of rain.
Cuz we don't thank these lungs enough
for air
or what our eyes can say...
But on this day
I know I'm grateful
for life
and what it brings
beyond today...

I knew you were the Sun to me
by the way
your warmth
drew my petals up
effortlessly.
I turned to face you,
but you were already
mid-embrace,
holding closed wounds
you had no way of knowing
were open in the first place...
I can tell you've been here before.

Extending your light
is most familiar to you.

You're rich in nourishment.
Without your presence,
the world would be sad and cold.

Non-existent...

Life itself
would end without you.

You are the source
of so many's healing
and I don't think
you're credited enough.
Without fail,
you rise to shine
day-in and day-out
without question...
Even when the clouds roll in,
you're still there.

...

Keeping distance during natural occurrence,
but safe-guarding,
nonetheless.

The Son of God...
You ask nothing in return for your service.

Strength.

You pour from an overflowing cup...
Only skilled souls
know the secret in that.
And you have yours, too...
I understand the power in your brightness,
but also
the power to mask,
using it.

Blinding.

Your insides radiate outwards,
yet there's sides
you hide away
from us to see...

Sometimes coverage
is deemed necessary
to protect from the heat
of your burning love.

You do nothing without passion.

You're intense,
but it's necessary.

...

I couldn't imagine
that someone who's responsible
for constant rotation
would be anything less than unwavering.

Grounded.

You bring us back to Earth.
You enlighten us with your words,
you shift our sinking worlds...
There'd be no balance without you.

So mister Sun,
I hope you know
we see you
and we feel you,
and we're thankful for your glow....
Especially from
this yellow flower
whom which the sun
stems growth.

You are here
to teach me,
we can be
both a house
and a home.
Nomadic to these vessels,
you remind me
the significance
of staying grounded.
How important
I must be
for an angel
to modify themselves
to the earth
for me.
Now here I tremble...
But this time,
spewing strength.
Memories of a late night
intertwines
with future thoughts
of early mornings...
Even the sun
and the moon
can't help but to spend
the rise of the day together...
and with you,
a lifetime.
Either in this one, or next...
When you find me,
plant your hand
on the left side of my chest.
**Feel my garden grow.**

# HOME

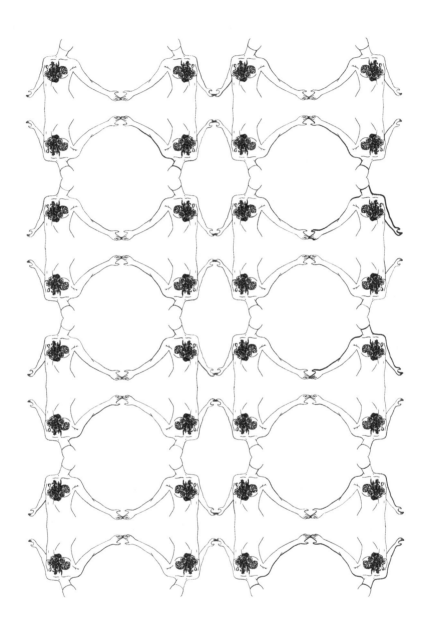

**Nothing seemed
to matter more**
than being
your favorite wallflower
and turning it
into the wallpaper
that decorated
your Home...

So this is how we start...
Dismantled,
entangled
and enchanted.
There is magic in your bones
and every stretch
triggers a spell.
You ward off
the un-necessities
to make room
for perfect peace.
You are both
the conductor
and the destroyer-
at your choosing,
of course.
And what better way
is there for you
to start the day
than in charge
and in power...

**You are a sorceress
of your own.
well-being.**

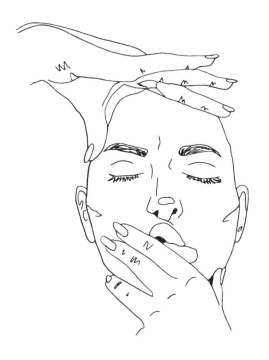

I'm taking time away to travel
and live with a nomadic heart.

**Home is not what it used to be,**
**yet I still long for it as a resting place.**

I will spend this time
finding adventure in myself,
collecting trinkets to bring back with me
and a new sense of wonder
and understanding
of the life
that moves around me.

There will be times
flu takes over my space
and engulfs me
in my Homesickness.
I will aid myself
by the Hand of the Healer
and keep pushing until
my purpose is fulfilled
as a traveling,
learning,
teacher.

Sometimes my ego
tries to keep me still.

Will there be a solid space to come back to?
Will the keeper of my Home
have found
another tenant to fill my place?

...

For now,
I wave "so long"
and wish you
safe housekeeping.

**May you keep the light on
and never burn out
as long as mine shines
for you,
Sweet Home...**

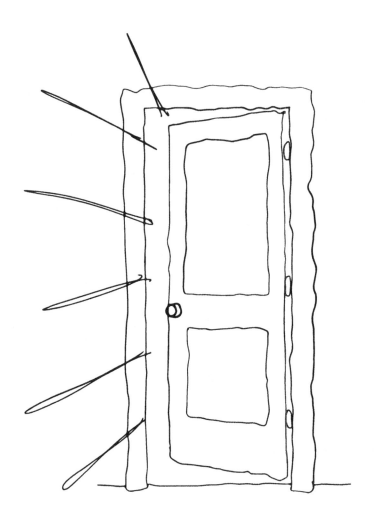

**If you leave what doesn't serve you,**
the doors for what does
will start swinging open
and shout your name
until you have
no other choice
but to run through it.

**To the men who've found a home in me:**

I've changed all my locks,
but the doors remain open.
We know our boundaries
so it's rare to have old visitors.

There's a mother in me that will always want to feed you
and I'm rather good at preparing a meal.

I find peace in knowing
my stove only burns
for present flame...

The floors creak.
There's history beneath your feet.

I'm constantly renovating,
changing and transforming-
I've painted my walls many times since I saw you last.

With a new season, my space needs renewal too...

There's still tallies from growth-charts at every door opening.
Though you've outgrown the frame,
there's still proof of your mark here.
And with that,
proof of when the growing stopped.

It never takes much time for move-out after that...

There's a security system now.
I'm heavy-guarded,
locked and loaded.
I have no intention to use my weapons,
but a heart-trigger tends to shoot with its eyes closed.

...

I'm still working on that.

But even then,
the foundation is the same...

You can take your cape off here,
your soul is safe with me.

I'm a good host and a natural caretaker.

Sometimes the lights flicker,
but there's always a spare bulb in the cupboard.
I'm over-prepared in this space...
By now you've been through
many or few new places
and you've taken your shoes off there.
I find joy in some of my practices resting in unfamiliar territory.

After all,
what a waste it'd have been
to leave your lessons here.
I wouldn't chase you down to return them...

So to all the men who've found a home in me,
your knick-knacks and picture frames
collected dust in empty rooms.
I hired a cleaner and Saged the house.
I found myself when the walls echoed back at me...

Thank you for your time here.
I promise to never forget...

But remember to leave your key.

Not everything I write
relates to me
**present,**

but the lessons
are a gift
from **past,**
towards **future.**

How much do you take away
from yourself
to fulfill needs of souls
outside of your own?
Do you give yourself permission
to decline energy withdrawals
or only exchange
with those able
to deposit after transaction?

What makes you think
you don't deserve
to be as full
as the cups you pour into?

Protect yourself.

**Stay filled
to the brim.**

**The chaos felt like home to me,**
built of restless thoughts
and poetry.

What a story this could be
if I let go of control
and trust destiny.

**I am aware
that all my guards
that are up
must come down,**
but for now
they keep me safe...

I am no stranger to vulnerability
but I am aware
not everyone
deserves yours.

The skill comes
in being able to acknowledge
where to give love
and hold access
warmly
and lovingly,
still.

Be gentle with yourself...

Remember that you
are a mirror.

**What you reflect
is beneath the frame;**
handle with care.

Soft around the edges,
you will be the force
that makes
the ground shake.

**Good morning little birdies
and the Sun
up in the sky...**
I've been braced
with no wings
so you remind me how to fly...

You run and jump,
you trust your gut,
you soar between the trees-
And everyday
whether warm or gray
you repeat
your routine.

The pretty songs
you sing and ring,
it's like
meditation to me.

You cleanse the air,
you do your share
of awakening
with morning.

Thank you for your conversation, early birds.

You make me feel at Home...
The kind of Home
that I miss
when I'm
in the places
I've always dreamed of...

The kind of Home
that I always want
to take with me.

**-Love found the Nomad**

**An Affirmation for transformation**

I am currently emerging
as a stronger
and more complete person...

I welcome all the triggers
that highlight the parts of me
that need healing.

I thank the darkness for
forcing a light out of me.

I appreciate my courage
to make tough decisions
so that I may become
more soft.

I acknowledge that what leaves my life
no longer serves me,
but I am still allowed to
mourn and recover
as needed.

I will find comfort
in un-comfortability
and it will make me whole.

Amen

My favorite form of self-love has been
obeying my vessel's need
to be accepted in its entirety...

To allow intimacy to flow from the inside-out...
To listen to my fingertips when it's time for them to speak.

To give in to relationship
when warm hands grasp my soul
and shut closed the cracks broken open.

Thank yourself for standing here today,
overcoming adversity and its consistency...

Thank your vessel
for being such a solid Home for your soul to relish in.
**We are in a season of deep gratitude,
dive in or be swallowed by the wave.**

**Before you go to sleep,
look at the moon
and think of me...**

I'll be your peace
amongst your dreams
and slowly you
will doze to sleep.

And in your head
inside your bed
the desires you have
will mold and mend
into the things
amidst your dreams
and turn to plans
you soon will see...

I painted across the stars
for you
the steps it takes
to see things through.

Is the sky
high enough
of a limit for you?

**I have been through
many lifetimes**
to stand here,
holding hands with grace
in this one...

So far,
this is my favorite form...

# AFTERWORD

Written between 2015 and 2020, this book is filled with some of my very first and very favorite pieces of poetry; from toxic relationships to healthy self-awareness, this book serves as a memory book and gentle timeline of my journey towards awakening...

If you know me personally, you know my perfectionist self wouldn't have been able to just throw together a body of work without it holding meanings within meanings within meanings of things and my ego is dying to take you behind the scenes of my brain.

The book is constructed like this:
There are 8 chapters to represent my life number (and first recollection of having a "favorite" number,) 8.
There are 6 illustrations in every chapter, alongside 23 pages worth of art and poetry within every chapter.
This represents my angel numbers, as well as my birthday 6/23...

While I don't feel so inclined in this after-word to include the many uses of double and triple entendres throughout my book, I can assure you there are more sprinkled surprises and hidden messages if you care to take the deep dive, yourself!
Also, don't even ask me how long this format took (and delayed my publishing date)...

Ok it was 3 extra months.


Now let me take a moment to highlight a few people for the completion of this work...

-This book was Illustrated by the lovely Jess Alba, and Formatted by the wonderful Haley Weigman. Thank you both for making me an author and my dreams come true.

-Thank you to my parents who produced a mirrored combination of their logic and creativity into the mind of a little curly-haired dreamer. I'm blessed and grateful for the incredible family you brought me into, and an additional shoutout to my brother and my (excessively large) extended family whom I love so much.

-Thank you to my Soulmate(s) who helped pave the way to myself. These come in many forms, from friends, to mentors, to people who are now just memories...
You know who you are <3

-Thank you to my Twin Flame whom I've loved through many past-lives, who found his way back to me and enhanced every atom of my being. This book wasn't ready until it met you.

-Thank you to my past lovers for the immense amount of heartbreak, love and teaching moments you gifted me with. I started writing out of pain and experimentation to comprehend confusion and it led me to finding a new way to communicate with myself, the world, and then God, through me and to me.

-Thank you to Asia and Kimora for reminding me the importance of staying young and dreaming big.

And thank you, reader and fellow poetry-lover for choosing my words to digest.
This has been the greatest march of vulnerability I have taken in my life thus-far and with this release, brings victory.

I am so happy to be here.
Come back anytime :)

Made in the USA
Coppell, TX
02 May 2021